ordinary GENUS

The Story of Albert Einstein

Stephanie Sammartino McPherson

Carolrhoda Books, Inc. / Minneapolis

For Dick, Jennifer, and Marianne,
with love and thanks

Text copyright © 1995 by Stephanie Sammartino McPherson

This book is available in two editions:
Library binding by Carolrhoda Books, Inc.
Soft cover by First Avenue Editions, 1997
c/o The Lerner Publishing Group
241 First Avenue North
Minneapolis, MN 55401 U.S.A.

Library of Congress Cataloging-in-Publication Data

McPherson, Stephanie Sammartino.
   Ordinary genius : the story of Albert Einstein / Stephanie
Sammartino McPherson.
      p.   cm. — (Trailblazers)
   Includes bibliographical references and index.
   Summary: Recounts the life of the scientist whose theories of relativity
revolutionized the way we look at space and time.
   ISBN 0-87614-788-0 (lib. bdg.)
   ISBN 1-57505-067-6 (pbk.)
   1. Einstein, Albert, 1879–1955—Juvenile literature. 2. Physicists—Biography—
Juvenile literature. [1. Einstein, Albert, 1879–1955. 2. Physicists.] I. Title.
QC16.E5M38 1995
530'.092—dc20
[B]   93-1408

Manufactured in the United States of America
4 5 6 7 8 9 – JR – 02 01 00 99 98 97

Contents

Author's Note

This book is about Albert Einstein's accomplishments and his impact on the world, both scientifically and politically. Although the facts of Einstein's life are well documented, sources occasionally differ on some of the details. In each instance, I have chosen the version that seemed to me most reliable. For help with the scientific portions of this book, particularly the special theory of relativity, I am indebted to Professor Priscilla Cushman of the University of Minnesota's Department of Physics. I would also like to thank my editor Vicki Revsbech for her support and advice and for suggesting a book about Albert Einstein in the first place.

This is the earliest known photograph of Albert Einstein, taken when he was five.

1

Different from the Start

Five-year-old Albert Einstein stared at his hand as if it held magic. Cupped in his palm was a small, round instrument with a glass cover and a jiggling needle. Albert's father called it a compass. Albert called it a mystery. No matter how he moved the compass, the needle always pointed to the north. Quietly Hermann Einstein watched his son. Albert was a chubby little boy with pale, round cheeks and thick, black hair that was usually messy. His bright brown eyes were wide with discovery.

Something was in the room with him, Albert realized—something he couldn't see or feel, but that acted on the compass just the same. Spellbound, Albert listened to his father explain magnetism, the strange force that made the compass needle point north. But nothing his father said made the invisible power seem less mysterious or wonderful. To many children the compass would have been just another toy. To Albert the compass was a miracle he would never forget.

But then Albert had always been different from other children. Born March 14, 1879, in Ulm, Germany, Albert hadn't even looked like other babies. As she cradled her new son in her arms, Pauline Einstein thought the back of his head looked strange. Other babies didn't have such large, pointed skulls. Was something wrong with Albert? Although the doctor told Pauline everything was fine, several weeks passed before the shape of Albert's head began to look right to her.

When Albert was one, his family moved to Munich, where his sister, Maja, was born a year later. Looking down at the tiny sleeping bundle, Albert was puzzled. Where were the baby's wheels? the disappointed two year old wanted to know. Albert had expected a baby sister to be something like a toy, and most of his toys had wheels.

Albert's parents were amused by his confusion. But any response at all would have delighted them. At an age when many children have lots to say, Albert seemed strangely backward. Hermann and Pauline wondered why he was so late in talking. Was their son developing normally? As Albert grew older, he continued to have trouble putting his thoughts into words. Even when he was nine years old, he spoke slowly, if he decided to say anything at all. Pauline and Hermann didn't know what to think.

But Albert was a good listener and a good thinker. Sometimes when he went hiking with his parents and go Einstien!

Maja, he thought about his father's compass and what it had revealed to him. The clear, open meadows were filled with more than the wind or the scent of flowers. They were also filled with magnetism. The very thought of it quickened Albert's pulse.

In the evenings, Albert's house rang with his father's merry voice and his mother's music. Pauline Einstein was a talented pianist who wanted her son to study music too. At age six, Albert began to take violin lessons. Like many young children, he didn't like to practice. But he wanted to please his mother, so he dutifully stuck his violin under his chin and played his scales.

There were so many things Albert would rather do than practice. He liked to daydream, play with blocks, and build houses out of playing cards. Sometimes his paper buildings reached fourteen stories high. He rarely played with other children, except Maja. Albert had a hard time making friends. He was quiet at school and didn't like sports. Other boys his age liked to play soldier and march stiffly around the playground. Albert wanted nothing to do with soldiers.

Once Albert had watched a military parade march through the streets of Munich. People cheered and ran to get a closer look at the soldiers in their bright uniforms and glossy boots. Something about the blank faces and rigid movements of the soldiers frightened Albert. The men were like parts of a vast machine. It seemed they could no longer think for themselves.

Albert made his parents promise that he would never have to be a soldier. But sometimes going to school

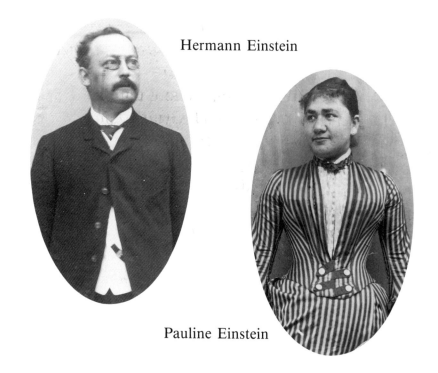

Hermann Einstein

Pauline Einstein

seemed just as bad. Although he was Jewish, Albert went to a Catholic elementary school because it was close to his home. His parents weren't religious, so they didn't mind that the school was Catholic. Albert didn't mind the Catholic part of his school either, but almost everything else about it bothered him.

At school Albert had to sit still for hours and wasn't allowed to ask questions. He had strict teachers who often hit their students with a ruler or yelled at them. Since Albert didn't like trouble, he tried to do everything the teachers wanted. But he had a hard time memorizing facts. He hated to read the same thing over and over again until he knew it by heart. Mathematics was better than other subjects because figuring out problems was easy and fun for Albert. But that didn't mean he was always right. Even in his favorite subject, he sometimes made careless mistakes.

Albert attended the Catholic school until he was ten. Then he went to the Luitpold Gymnasium for high school. The high school teachers weren't any better than the ones at the elementary school. Once Albert gave a poorly done paper to his Greek teacher. Instead of showing him how to improve it, the teacher shook his head in disgust and told Albert he would never amount to anything.

Luckily at home Albert had someone who understood him much better than his teachers. That was his uncle Jakob, who lived with the Einstein family. Uncle Jakob saw how much Albert enjoyed working with numbers. One day he decided to introduce Albert to algebra. Algebra problems can be long and complicated, but Uncle Jakob made them into a game. Albert was so good at algebra that soon he was ready for a more advanced kind of math and a new teacher.

Max Talmud was one of Albert's first friends. He was ten years older than Albert, but when they got talking about their interests, the age difference didn't matter much. A struggling Jewish medical student, Max had an invitation to dine with the Einsteins every Thursday.

One day Max brought a geometry book for Albert when he came to dinner. Geometry is a kind of math that involves shapes, such as circles, squares, and rectangles. Twelve-year-old Albert was delighted. The book captured his imagination and became his window into a whole new world of logic, beauty, and harmony. Albert considered geometry a kind of miracle, like the compass. Every week when Max came to dinner, Albert proudly showed him the problems he had completed. Rapidly Albert went through the entire book. Then he set out to teach himself an even more advanced form of mathematics called calculus. Soon he could no longer discuss his progress with Max. Albert's mathematical ability was far beyond that of his astonished friend.

Now Albert and Max spent their time talking about philosophy and the science books Max brought Albert to read. Brightly colored and simply written, the popular volumes were unlike any books Albert had ever seen. They introduced him to such fascinating topics as electricity, gravity, atoms, and stars—things Albert didn't get much chance to learn about in school. But he wanted to know more. So much of the world was a mystery. The more people learned, the more it seemed there was yet to learn. Sometimes Albert thought the whole world was like a giant riddle. He longed to find some answers.

Albert's parents were glad he liked science. His mother was also happy with his musical skills. After he discovered Mozart's sonatas, Albert came to love the violin. He didn't even mind practicing anymore.

Hermann and Pauline Einstein worried less about their quiet, clever son. But there were other concerns that weighed heavily on them. The electrical factory they owned with Uncle Jakob was not doing well. Larger companies were beginning to take over the market for electrical equipment in Germany. Albert's father and uncle had a hard time finding buyers for their products. Finally they decided to sell their business and open a new factory in Milan, Italy.

To his great disappointment, fifteen-year-old Albert was left behind to finish school when the family moved. Albert's father settled him in a comfortable boarding-house and told him to study hard for his diploma.

After his family left, however, a diploma didn't seem important to Albert. He continued to do well in math and science, but he didn't like most of his other subjects. School had never been much fun. Now it was almost unbearable. Albert was restless and angry. Sometimes he slumped in his seat and gazed moodily into space. If he wasn't interested in something, he didn't try to hide his boredom. But if he was interested, that was almost worse. Then Albert might ask questions the teachers couldn't answer. The teachers hated the sarcastic way Albert smiled when they tried to ignore him. They thought he was making fun of them. The other students thought so too, and they couldn't wait to see what Albert would do next.

All Albert wanted to do was leave school and be with his family. His father's letters made Italy sound like a wonderful place. Albert wanted to see the olive groves and feel the sunshine for himself. He wanted to talk with his parents and laugh with Maja. The more he thought of his family in warm, colorful Italy, the more determined he became not to bother about a diploma. Soon he had a plan.

Albert told his family doctor how lonely and nervous

Although Albert was a loner at school, he felt free to laugh, argue, and talk about whatever he wanted with his sister, Maja. This photo was taken when Albert was about fourteen and Maja about twelve.

he was. He complained about not feeling well and convinced the doctor to write a letter saying he needed a long vacation from school. Just having the medical excuse in his pocket made Albert feel free. He paid even less attention to his teachers. Finally his homeroom teacher asked to see him privately. He expelled Albert, telling him no one in the class respected the teachers when he was around. Albert had not even had a chance to use his excuse! It was one thing to arrange his own escape, but it was quite another to be asked to leave. Insulted and relieved at the same time, Albert prepared to join his family in Italy.

II

On His Own

Almost as soon as his train crossed the Alps, Albert was enchanted by Italy. He could hardly wait to explore the countryside and meet the people. But first he had to promise his parents he would do some studying too. Someday he would return to school, Albert told them, but he never wanted to live in Germany again. In fact, he wanted to give up his German citizenship. Hermann and Pauline thought this was going too far. Although they didn't make Albert enroll in school, they wouldn't let him renounce his citizenship.

In sunny Italy, Albert's old anger fell off him like a cloak. Up hills and down valleys he rambled in search of adventure. Albert came to love the Italian people. With their lively manner and quick sympathy, they seemed so different from the formal, serious Germans he had known. Albert's wavy, dark hair and brilliant brown eyes made him look almost Italian himself. That was fine with

Albert at sixteen

him. Italy was a better home to Albert than Germany had ever been.

Even though Albert became more outgoing in Italy, he still liked to be alone. Sometimes strange thoughts came to him as he walked by himself in the sunshine or watched the stars come out at night. Albert thought about light traveling from the sun or stars to reach his eyes. How did light make that long trip through space? Experienced scientists had never been able to answer this question, but Albert wrote down some ideas of his own. This was a project he would never have been allowed to do for school—the teachers wouldn't have understood it.

But Albert knew his ideas were just the beginning. He still had lots of thinking to do.

Albert's father was doing some thinking too. The Einstein brothers' business had begun to fail again, and they were struggling to keep it open. Hermann Einstein began to lose patience with Albert. He finally told his son he could no longer support him and that Albert would have to take up a profession.

Albert's father thought his son would make a good electrical engineer. He wanted to send him to Zurich, Switzerland, to the famous Polytechnic School. At sixteen, Albert was two years younger than most of the school's students. He had never graduated from high school. But if he passed a special test, he would be allowed to attend.

Albert realized his Italian vacation had to end sometime. Obediently he set off for Switzerland. But he didn't study very hard for what he knew would be a difficult test. Although he scored brilliantly in physics and mathematics, Albert failed almost every other subject. There was nothing for him to do but follow a friendly professor's advice. He enrolled in high school in the nearby town of Aarau, Switzerland.

From the very beginning, Albert realized his new high school was different from his German school. The classes were relaxed and friendly. He could say what he liked and ask any questions he wished. If the teachers couldn't answer, they weren't angry. Instead they were delighted with Albert's sharp mind. They encouraged him to explore the physics, chemistry, and zoology rooms. Albert

On a class hiking trip in the beautiful but treacherous Alps, Albert lost his footing and began to slide down a steep slope. A quick-thinking friend saved Albert's life by thrusting out a climbing stick for him to grab.

was still the stubborn young man he had been in Germany. He still smiled sarcastically at times. But he respected his teachers, and they respected him.

The teacher Albert boarded with welcomed him like a member of the family. Professor Winteler liked to go hiking through the mountains with his seven children and his students. Striding through the open countryside, enjoying the scenery and the brisk breeze, Albert felt right at home. Sometimes he joined in his new friends' laughter. Other times he followed his own thoughts like a wandering stream until they led him back to the same question.

What would it be like to ride through space on a beam of light? At that time scientists believed light traveled about 140,460 miles per second. Today we know that light goes even faster, at 186,282 miles per second. But Albert wasn't concerned with measuring the actual speed. He was more interested in what he would see. How would the universe look to someone keeping pace with a beam of light? Over and over again, Albert played the impossible adventure in his mind.

The year he spent in Aarau was one of the happiest of Albert's life. Now that he'd come to love Switzerland and Italy, he was more determined than ever not to return to Germany. Once more he told his parents that he did not want to be German. Hermann and Pauline Einstein saw their son was growing up. He was living away from home and studying hard. Perhaps it was time for him to make his own decisions. Albert's father promised to write a letter to the German authorities about his son's wishes. Not long afterward, on January 28, 1896, Albert became a boy without a country.

By the time Albert was accepted at the Polytechnic School later that year, his parents had accepted another of his plans. Albert had learned what a difference good teachers could make to their students. He decided to become a science teacher instead of an electrical engineer. At last everything seemed to be falling into place for Albert.

It should have been an exciting time to study physics. New discoveries were being made that seemed to challenge long-accepted ideas about time and space. Albert wanted to know more about these developments, but the latest findings weren't taught in his classes. Although the Polytechnic School had a fine reputation, Albert found the teaching to be practical and dull. He wanted to go far beyond the concepts his teachers talked about. Already he felt driven to discover how the universe was put together. Often when he should have been in class, Albert stayed at his boardinghouse, studying the new ideas on his own.

Albert's teachers didn't like him any more than he liked them. They thought he was rebellious and lazy. It was the same old story of Albert's school days in Munich. Albert was bored and he didn't care who knew it. He refused to cooperate unless he had to. But this time Albert managed to stay in school. And this time he had friends to encourage him and keep him from being lonely.

Mileva Maric and Marcel Grossmann knew a very different Albert from the one the teachers saw. Mileva and Marcel considered Albert a brilliant, witty, and original young man—someone who was fascinating and fun to be with. But he also seemed to need someone to look after him. For such an intelligent person, Albert could be surprisingly absentminded. He skipped meals; he dressed carelessly. Often he forgot the key to his lodging.

Mileva reminded Albert to eat regular meals and to budget the small monthly allowance his mother's wealthy relatives sent him. She was a serious young woman and a hardworking student, but she enjoyed Albert's happy-go-lucky ways. Some people felt the students were drawn to each other simply because they were such opposites. But when Albert was especially forgetful, Mileva sometimes became angry. Then Albert would make silly faces at her, tell jokes, and tease her until she smiled again.

In spite of their differences, Mileva and Albert had a great deal in common. Mileva, who was the only woman in Albert's class, cared about physics, mathematics, and music—the same things that mattered to Albert. She played the piano for Albert and listened eagerly to his ideas. The more time they spent together, the more deeply the young students came to care about each other. Albert began to dream of sharing his life with Mileva.

Marcel Grossmann believed in Albert as much as Mileva did. Marcel was a better student than Albert, but he recognized in his friend a genius that he himself lacked. Several days after he met Albert, he remarked that his new friend would one day be a great man. Happy to help him, Marcel took detailed notes of every lecture and loaned them to Albert before tests.

Although school was a disappointment, Albert did learn something important in Zurich that stayed with him the rest of his life. He learned to sail. Zurich was surrounded by beautiful lakes. Some of Albert's best thoughts came to him as he sat far from shore in a rocking boat. He usually carried a little notebook in his pocket, and when the breeze died down, he would jot down ideas. As soon as the wind began to fill the sails, Albert was ready to be a sailor again.

Music was another activity that Albert found both exciting and relaxing. One day in his boardinghouse, he heard the sound of a piano sonata coming through the window. Grabbing his violin, Albert ran outdoors and followed the sound up the stairs of a neighboring house. He barged into the room and urged the startled woman

Marcel Grossmann helped Albert get his first job and later helped him with the mathematics of the general theory of relativity.

to keep playing. Then he positioned his violin to accompany her. It was the first of many musical sessions they shared.

But as graduation approached, Albert had less and less time for music and sailing. Would Marcel's notes be enough to get him through final exams? Could months of frantic study make up for four years of neglect? For once Albert made his classes the most important thing in his life.

Albert's efforts paid off. In 1900, at the age of twenty-one, he received his diploma from the Polytechnic School. But he soon discovered that his troubles were far from over.

Albert had hoped for a teaching position at the Polytechnic School. New graduates were usually offered a beginning post under an established professor. But none of the professors wanted to work with Albert. None of them wanted to help him find another job either. After graduation, Albert's relatives cut off his allowance. More than anything else, Albert and Mileva longed to be married, but without regular employment, Albert could not support a wife.

Albert had no job, no money, and worst of all, no heart for science. His final months at school had been so stressful that he even lost interest in his personal studies. For more than a year, he didn't even want to think about science. Instead Albert thought mostly about finding employment. Finally Marcel suggested that Albert apply for a job at the Swiss Patent Office in Berne. Studying other people's inventions certainly wasn't the kind of work for which Albert had been trained. But at that point, any job looked good to him. Albert had discovered it wasn't enough to be smart. He had to be patient and willing to compromise. He had to get along with people in authority. And somehow he had to support himself.

Sitting across from the patent director during his two-hour job interview, Albert felt hopeful but humble. Friedrich Haller asked lots of questions that Albert couldn't answer. But the director saw that Albert was bright and willing to work hard. In the end, he decided that the eager young man would do just fine. At last Albert had his first permanent job.

III

The Secrets of the Universe

Albert was good at his new job. He enjoyed poring over the plans for inventions such as new cameras or improved popguns to see if they were workable and original. Soon he learned to go to the very heart of an idea and express it in short, clear sentences. This was a skill that also helped him with the scientific papers he was trying to write. Albert had not given up on physics. He was hoping to earn a Ph.D. degree from the University of Zurich. But more than that, he wanted knowledge for its own sake. He was passionately curious about almost everything. The patent office gave him the time and security he needed to think about scientific matters.

Sometimes between inventions, Albert would grab a scrap of paper to scribble down his ideas. He was still fascinated by things that most people take for granted, like light and space and time. Whenever the patent director walked by, Albert would shove his paper into a desk

Albert, Mileva, and Hans Albert, 1904

drawer. But soon it would come out again. Albert's ideas filled every spare moment of his day.

Outwardly Albert's life changed dramatically in the next few years. Shortly after Albert started his new job, his father died. A few months later, in January 1903, Albert and Mileva were married. Their son Hans Albert was born in 1904. Albert was thrilled, but even fatherhood couldn't distract him from physics. If he rocked the baby's cradle with one hand, he was often holding a science book in the other.

Just as he had in college, Albert liked to discuss his ideas with his friends. One of them, Michele Angelo Besso, sat next to Albert in the patent office. As they walked home together in the evening, Albert and Michele Angelo talked about light and the way it related to speed and motion. Two other friends, Maurice Solovine and Conrad Habicht, visited Albert at his apartment to talk about physics and philosophy. The famous clock in the town square usually struck the early morning hours before their lively discussions broke up.

During those first creative years, Albert Einstein tackled a wide range of issues. For instance, he was interested in molecules, tiny particles of matter too small to be seen with our eyes alone. In 1905 there were no microscopes powerful enough to let scientists see molecules. Some scientists didn't even believe that they existed. But Einstein's studies had convinced him that molecules were real. The question was how to prove this.

Then Einstein thought about a problem that had been bothering scientists for years—the way pollen behaves in a liquid. Pollen is a dustlike substance produced by plants. When scientists added it to a liquid, the tiny grains never stopped moving. Instead of sinking or coming to rest somewhere in the liquid, they zigzagged back and forth, up and down. This movement was called Brownian motion, after the man who discovered it. What was making the pollen move? Einstein wrote a paper that proved that molecules of water were bumping into the grains of pollen and moving them. Not only did Einstein prove molecules exist, he solved the mystery of Brownian motion at the same time.

Even while he was thinking about molecules, Einstein couldn't stop wondering about light. Most scientists believed that light was made up of waves moving smoothly and steadily through space, something like waves of water rippling outward from a stone thrown into a pond. But Einstein believed that light was more than just waves. Light was also made up of tiny particles of energy called quanta. He said that sometimes light acts like a wave and sometimes it acts like a line of particles.

Einstein's surprising conclusion solved a problem that scientists had been wondering about for years. In experiments, tiny particles called electrons were knocked off a sheet of metal when the metal was struck by a beam of light. This was called the photoelectric effect. It really had scientists puzzled because even though a wave of light could jiggle electrons off the metal, the electrons behaved more like they had been knocked off by a stream of particles. Einstein said that was exactly what had happened and that the stream of particles was made up of bits of light. At last there was an explanation for the photoelectric effect.

Albert Einstein found beauty in mathematics and natural laws the way most people find it in a flower or a sunset. Sometimes he would look up from his work in triumph and exclaim over what a beautiful solution he had found. Other times he grew excited before the conclusion was in. "I hope this works out, the answer would be lovely," he might confide to his friends.

But Albert was often frustrated too. Whenever he ran into difficulties, he grew tense and anxious. He paced the floor or pulled on his thick, springy hair or clenched his cigar tightly between his lips. Mileva listened to Albert's ideas and double-checked the arithmetic in his equations. Although she was happy with her husband, sometimes she wished he had more time to simply relax with her and the baby. Occasionally she wanted to talk of other things besides science. Albert was so absent-minded when he worked on physics that he didn't always notice Mileva's feelings.

Like a man obsessed, Albert continued to think about light and the way it passes through space. Proving the existence of molecules and explaining the photoelectric effect were big accomplishments, but they weren't enough. Albert knew there was an important connection to be made between light, space, and time, but he couldn't quite tie all his ideas together into a theory. Sometimes he thought he would go crazy trying to come up with the thread of logic he needed.

One evening Albert turned to Michele Angelo and sadly

told him that he had decided to give up on the whole theory. But the next morning, Albert woke up thinking about his theory again. Light always travels at the same speed—Albert's own words echoed in his mind. This was something he had already discussed with Michele Angelo. But suddenly Albert knew the idea was even more important than he'd imagined. The speed of light was the key to the whole mystery. Excited, Albert reached for a pencil and some paper. Soon he was lost in his own thoughts.

Einstein's idea sounds simple enough until you compare light to other things that move. Most objects move at different speeds, depending on how you look at them. For example, you push a toy race car across the floor and measure the speed at 2 miles per hour. What if the same car is pushed across the floor of a train going 100 miles per hour? Is the car going 2 miles per hour or 102 miles per hour? The earth is also traveling through space. Do you add in the speed of the earth too? How fast is the toy car really going?

There is no one answer. According to Einstein, all the measurements are correct. If you are on the train, the toy seems to go 2 miles per hour. If you are on the ground, it passes you at 102 miles per hour. And if you could watch the scene from outer space, you would have to add in the speed of the earth too. All the speeds depend on, or are relative to, where you are.

But Einstein said that light was different. No matter where you are or how fast you are going, light would always travel at the same speed, which we now know is

This toy car is traveling at 2 miles per hour (mph).

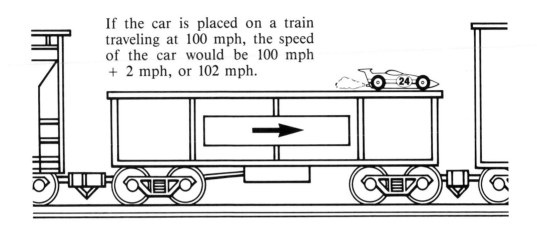

If the car is placed on a train traveling at 100 mph, the speed of the car would be 100 mph + 2 mph, or 102 mph.

The speed of light is 186,282 miles per second (mps).

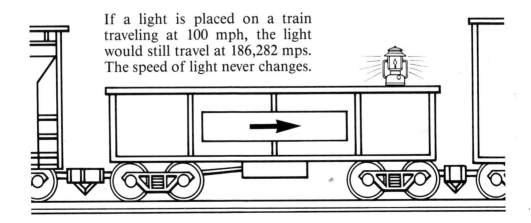

If a light is placed on a train traveling at 100 mph, the light would still travel at 186,282 mps. The speed of light never changes.

186,282 miles per second. To see what this means, think of a beam of light shining from a train traveling at 100 miles per hour. To someone outside the train, wouldn't the beam be traveling at 186,282 miles per second plus the speed of the train? Einstein said no. The beam of light was nothing like the toy race car. The speed of light is always the same; it is never relative.

The next five weeks were hectic ones for Einstein. He spent every spare moment working out the mathematics of the new ideas he called his special theory of relativity. His conclusion about the speed of light had only been the beginning. He saw that there was indeed a connection between light, space, and time. Einstein's calculations told him that since the speed of light can never change, our measurements of time and space must change. Like the speed of the toy car on the train, time and space are relative—they change according to where you are.

In our everyday life, the changes are too small for us to notice. We can be sitting at home or flying in an airplane, and our watches still show the same time. But when an object approaches the speed of light, some very strange things begin to happen. Let's say a spaceship is whizzing by earth near the speed of light. If earthbound observers could see the inside of the ship, they would think everything on board (including the clocks) had slowed down—like a movie running in slow motion. But the space crew wouldn't see anything wrong on the ship. Time would pass for them in the same way as always. In fact to them, time seems to slow down on earth. So who is correct—the space travelers or the people on earth? They both are. They are simply looking at each other from different places, or frames of reference. It doesn't matter who's really moving. What matters is that the two frames of reference—the earth and the spaceship—are moving in relation to each other.

Now let's imagine an identical spaceship sitting on a launchpad on earth. The people beside it think the ship streaking by in space is shorter. The space crew thinks the ship on the ground is shorter. But both spaceships were built to be exactly the same size! Even stranger, both groups of people are correct. It's their frames of reference that make the difference.

The space travelers and earth observers can't even agree on which ship is more massive. Mass is a measure of the amount of force, or push, it takes to move an object. When something has large mass, a large force is needed to move it. An object with smaller mass doesn't need as big a push. As the spaceship gets closer to the speed of light, a larger and larger force is needed to make it go even faster.

Has the flying ship gained mass? Is it heavier? That's the way it would seem to people on earth if they could weigh it. People on the spaceship wouldn't see it that way at all. To them, the other ship (and everything on earth) would gain mass. This doesn't mean that either spaceship really grows bigger or heavier. The two space-ships simply become harder to move from each other's frames of reference. When a spaceship goes fast enough, it becomes so hard to move that no force can increase

Einstein at his desk
at the patent office,
1905

its speed further. There is an upper limit to how fast
anything can go.

This brought Einstein back to the same question he
had been asking since he was sixteen. What would it be
like to travel as fast as light? Now he knew there was
no real answer to his question. No spaceship and nothing
in the universe can go as fast as light.

These were incredible ideas. Einstein knew that most
scientists would find it hard to accept that time, space,
and mass change according to how you look at them.
But he had worked out all the details mathematically and

knew he was correct. One by one Einstein wrote up his theories for publication: his explanation of Brownian motion, his ideas about light and the photoelectric effect, and his special theory of relativity. In September 1905, all three articles appeared in the *Annalen der Physik,* an important physics journal. Not only was this a turning point in Einstein's life, it was an equally big milestone in the history of physics.

But Einstein knew there was still more to do. He kept thinking about mass and energy. How are they related to each other? Then he made another amazing discovery. Mass and energy are the same thing. This means that anything that has mass can be turned into energy.

Einstein expressed this idea in what has been called the most famous equation of the twentieth century: $E = mc^2$. It means that if you multiply the mass of a body by the speed of light, then multiply your answer by the speed of light again, you will know how much energy is locked inside that object. Because the speed of light is so great, a very small amount of matter can produce a very large amount of energy.

But Einstein's special theory of relativity said nothing about how to get the energy out of an object. He wasn't interested in putting this knowledge to practical use. He didn't want to make machines or build inventions. For him it was a privilege and joy just to discover something new about the universe.

IV

Einstein's Happiest Thought

By the end of 1905, twenty-six-year-old Albert had his Ph.D. and a growing circle of scientific admirers. But he didn't have a teaching job, and his daily life had hardly changed at all. He still rose early and walked to the patent office, carrying his lunch in a brown paper bag. He still snatched odd minutes from his job for his own private work, and he still juggled his time at home between physics and his family. Albert split wood for the stove, played with his son, and studied science at night.

Sometimes Albert even found time to daydream. One day a very strange thought came to him. He realized that a person falling freely through the air would not feel the weight of his or her own body. The words seemed to flash into his mind from nowhere. Looking back Albert called this the happiest thought of his life.

Einstein's "happy thought" wouldn't seem important to most people. But it led him to some interesting conclusions. If falling makes a person feel weightless, what would it feel like to travel upward moving faster and faster, or accelerating, through space? Einstein imagined an elevator in outer space. Since accelerating away from earth is the opposite of falling freely toward earth, Einstein decided that the accelerating person would feel a downward tug. The tug would be the same as the feeling of gravity, the force that pulls things toward the earth's surface. Einstein figured that the faster the person accelerated away from earth, the stronger the downward tug would be.

Einstein called this relationship between gravity and acceleration the "equivalence principle." He meant that accelerating through space produces the same result as gravity. But Einstein wasn't nearly through with his happy

The Einstein family lived at 49 Kramgasse (the second apartment from the left) in Berne. At the end of the street is Berne's famous clock tower.

thought. Soon he was working on a whole new theory.

Most scientists were still thinking about Albert's older theory. With his growing reputation, Albert felt it was about time he began his academic career. He wanted to be a professor, but first he had to be a *privatdozent,* someone who gave lectures for a small fee. In 1908 he became a *privatdozent* at the University of Berne. Because he kept his job at the patent office, Albert had to schedule his lectures at odd hours. His first talks were attended only by three or four students, including his friend Michele Angelo. Occasionally Maja, now a student at the university, would stop by to hear what her brother had to say. By Albert's second term, he had only one student left. Meanwhile, outside the classroom, Einstein's ideas were receiving more and more attention. Finally in 1909, Albert was offered a position as an associate professor at the University of Zurich.

Albert and Mileva returned to the city where they had met. They moved into an apartment at the foot of a great mountain called the Zurichberg. Albert continued to develop his gravity theory and to lecture, while Mileva took in boarders to help make ends meet. Albert didn't make any more money than he had as a patent officer, but his expenses were greater since he was expected to attend social events and entertain other professors in his home. Although this worried Mileva, Albert wasn't concerned about money and even joked about what he couldn't afford.

In July 1910, Mileva gave birth to a second son, Eduard, nicknamed Tede or Tedel. Albert called his sons *die*

Maja Einstein at eighteen

Bärchen, or "the little bears." By now Hans Albert was a lively little boy who liked to play with his father and watch him make toys. Albert designed imaginative playthings from simple items like match boxes and string. A small cable car he made became one of Hans Albert's most prized toys.

Like his father, Albert took his family for outings in the country. And like his mother, he often talked to his oldest son about music, which continued to be important to Albert. Whenever Albert's work was going poorly, he liked to play his violin. Sometimes the answer to a problem would come to him right in the middle of a melody. Then Albert would write down the solution, check his work carefully, and walk about happily whistling and sharing his excitement with anyone willing to listen.

Albert's friendliness and sense of humor made him a favorite with his students in Zurich, even though at first they thought him a little strange. Albert came to his first lecture poorly dressed in pants that were too short. His only notes were on a single small scrap of paper. But within minutes, the students knew they had a very special teacher—one who cared about physics and cared about them. Albert welcomed questions and often invited students to a nearby cafe or to his home to continue classroom discussions.

It seemed that Albert had everything he could want—happy children, a promising career, beautiful surroundings, fine lakes for sailing. Then he received another job offer that seemed to promise even more. Albert was invited to be a full professor at the German University in Prague, Austria-Hungary. He would earn a higher salary, but the university's large library was more important to Albert than the money. He believed he would make swifter progress on his research in Prague.

Professionally, Prague turned out to be a fine place for Albert. He met talented scientists, advanced his new theory, and continued teaching. Some of his lectures were better than others because Albert found it easier to speak on the topics that excited him most. Whatever they discussed, however, Albert enjoyed talking to his students and would interrupt his own work at any moment to help them.

But in spite of the satisfaction he took in his work,

Albert felt uneasy in the city. Three groups of people lived in Prague—Germans, Czechs, and Jews. Suspicious of each other, they stayed apart as much as possible. Many of the Germans acted as if they were more important or better than others, and both the Czechs and the Germans were prejudiced against the large Jewish population. Albert was outraged. For a while as a child, he had been interested in the Jewish religion. Now he began thinking about the Jewish people. For the first time in his life, he sought out Jewish friends and took part in Jewish social and intellectual gatherings.

Like her husband, Mileva felt uncomfortable in Prague. Having a maid and electricity in her apartment couldn't make up for the feeling that she didn't belong in the city. She was beginning to feel dissatisfied with her life and with Albert. But less than two years after the Einsteins moved to Prague, Albert was preparing to return with his family to Zurich.

Twelve years had passed since Albert's professors at the Polytechnic School had turned their backs on him after graduation. Now Albert was thirty-three years old, and the school couldn't wait to get him back as a teacher. Remembering his happy days in Aarau, Albert was glad that his sons would attend Swiss schools. Mileva was also delighted with the move.

At the Polytechnic School in Zurich, Albert gave young scientists the kind of education he himself had wanted in college. He put a great deal of effort into his lectures and tried to cover all the latest developments in physics, but he was never afraid to tell his students, "I don't

Mileva Einstein with Eduard, age four, and Hans Albert, age ten

know." Professors and students from both the Poly-technic School and the University of Zurich flocked to attend his weekly meetings.

In the summer of 1913, two well-known scientists, Max Planck and Walther Nernst, came to Zurich with an of-fer for Albert. Would he consider an appointment in Germany at the University of Berlin? Albert would be able to budget his time any way he liked. He could give frequent lectures or he could spend most of his time on research.

It was an excellent offer, but Albert needed time to think. Planck and Nernst decided to take a scenic train ride into the Swiss mountains while Albert made up his mind. Grinning, Albert told them that if they saw him carrying a red rose when they returned, his answer was yes. A white rose meant no.

After they left, Albert thought about living in Berlin. Almost eighteen years had passed since he had given up his German citizenship. He was happy in Switzerland and knew Mileva wouldn't want to move again. Lately Albert and Mileva had been disagreeing more often. The move might put more of a strain on their already troubled marriage. But then Albert thought about the opportunities he would have in Berlin. What should he do? As the time approached for Planck and Nernst to return, Albert went out to find a red rose.

V

Proof from the Sky

Albert had tears in his eyes as he watched his sons prepare to board the train. Several weeks had passed since his family moved to Berlin in April 1914. Now Mileva was taking Hans Albert and Eduard back to Switzerland for a visit. They were only supposed to be gone for a few weeks. But Albert knew Mileva was unhappy in Germany. He felt uncertain about the future.

The outbreak of World War I settled the matter. On June 28, 1914, Archduke Francis Ferdinand of Austria-Hungary was assassinated by a terrorist from Serbia. Within weeks most of Europe was at war. Suddenly it wasn't safe for Albert's family to return to Germany. Months later when they could have traveled more safely, Mileva and the children stayed in Switzerland. Albert missed his sons, but their absence left him more time to develop his theory of gravity.

Albert in his study in Berlin in 1916, the year his general theory
of relativity was published

Einstein needed all the time he could get. He was working on some very difficult equations. He wanted to prove that light doesn't always travel in a straight line, but can be bent by gravity. It was a remarkable claim. Other scientists would want more than mathematical proof that it was true. How could Einstein demonstrate his idea in the real world?

If Einstein's idea was correct, then the sun's gravity should change the course of light rays from distant stars as those rays pass the sun. But we can't see those light rays, or stars, from earth because the sun is so bright it blocks them out. What about during a solar eclipse? wondered Einstein. When an eclipse occurs, the moon passes in front of the sun and temporarily blocks the light of the sun from earth. Astronomers could photograph stars near the sun and compare them with photos of the same stars taken at a different season when they appeared in the night sky. If the stars seemed to shift position in the sky, it would mean that their light had been bent by the sun's gravity.

When Albert first came to Berlin, it seemed that his new theory might be tested soon. A solar eclipse was to take place in August 1914. One of Albert's friends, the astronomer Erwin Finlay-Freundlich, was planning to lead an expedition to Russia, where there would be the best views of the eclipse on earth. But the war put an end to Albert's hopes for the expedition.

Cut off from his children, horrified by the German enthusiasm for war, Albert felt very alone. Even his fellow scientists in Berlin seemed anxious to join the war effort.

They designed airplanes, investigated poison gas, and served as military consultants. They also signed a statement called the Manifesto of the 93, which claimed that Germany wasn't responsible for the war.

Albert hated the war and felt that Germany really was to blame. For years Germany had been looking for a way to expand its boundaries and prove its military strength. It had encouraged Austria-Hungary to declare war on Serbia. Then it had welcomed the excuse to declare war on Serbia's allies Russia and France. The German army had gone on to break international law by invading the neutral country of Belgium.

Instead of signing the Manifesto of the 93, Albert wrote a statement of his own with another professor, George Nicolai. The two men called on educated men and women of all countries to forget their differences and work together for peace. They hoped that someday a league of Europeans would help promote worldwide friendship.

This was the first time Albert had publicly taken a political stand. He hoped his statement would encourage people to rethink their views on the war. But only four people signed the statement, including Einstein and Nicolai themselves. Disappointed and bewildered, Einstein wondered what was the matter with everyone. The war made no sense to him at all.

What did make sense to Albert were his equations and his gravity theory. What is gravity? he kept asking himself. This was a question most scientists thought had been answered long ago. They believed gravity was a force that pulled on objects the way a magnet pulls on metal.

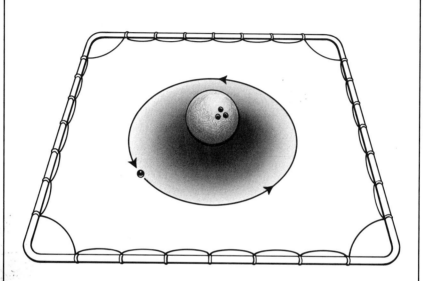

Einstein said that gravity is really curved space. To get an idea of what this means, imagine a flat, elastic surface like a trampoline. Now imagine a bowling ball placed on top. The ball makes a deep dent in the trampoline. In this simple model, the trampoline is space and the ball is the sun. Gravity is the dent that causes objects near the bowling ball to fall towards the ball's surface. Now suppose a marble is set whirling in a rapid circle around the bowling ball. If it is traveling fast enough, the marble will not fall against the ball. But it can't escape either. The marble is trapped, just as the planets are trapped in their orbits around the sun. Of course, three-dimensional space is much more complicated than the flat surface of a trampoline.

Einstein's equations showed that gravity was much stranger than this. Einstein believed that large bodies, like the stars and planets, caused space to curve around them. Gravity is really curved space, he declared. It's even harder to understand that time also curves around a large object like the sun and that space and time cannot be separated. In fact they are so closely related that physicists often combine the names into a single word: spacetime.

Albert described spacetime mathematically in ten of the hardest equations ever worked out by anyone. He called his new work the general theory of relativity. It explained more about the way the universe works than his special theory of relativity did.

When Albert worked on his calculations, he could forget for a few enchanted hours that a war was going on. But there was no forgetting when he picked up a newspaper or even when he thought about dinner. Food was very scarce in wartime Germany. Meat and sugar were not available. Bread was rarely fit to eat. Luckily for Albert, he had an uncle in Berlin with enough food to share.

At his uncle's house, Albert enjoyed the companionship of his cousin Elsa. The friendly, fun-loving little girl whom Albert remembered from his boyhood in Munich was now divorced and had two nearly grown daughters. In spite of the war, she was as good-natured and amusing as ever. She knew how to make Albert smile and relax in a way that his more serious wife had not. She joked with him and shared memories of happier times. The one thing she could not do was discuss physics as Mileva had done, but neither she nor Albert seemed to mind.

Elsa did understand that physics was the most important thing in Albert's life. She knew he struggled with and rejoiced in his work. When his general theory of relativity was finally published in 1916, Elsa was happy for her cousin.

But seeing his work in print didn't mean Einstein was done with it. He continued to think about his theory. What did his new ideas suggest about the universe? Was there an end to space or did it go on forever? In 1917 Einstein tackled that difficult question in another paper. He said the universe was like the surface of a giant balloon. You can't tell where the balloon's surface begins or ends, but it doesn't stretch on forever. It has boundaries.

Today we know that the universe is more like a giant balloon that is still being blown up. The stars and planets are moving away from each other as the universe gets larger and larger. Einstein's paper may not have been completely correct, but it was the beginning of the modern science of cosmology, the study of the beginning and end of the universe.

Albert was so caught up in his ideas that he would work through mealtime and never miss it until his stomach rumbled with hunger or a friend plunked a plate of food on top of his equations. Dreamily Albert would continue to eat until somebody stopped him. He would stay up half the night, then sleep half the morning unless someone arrived to rouse him.

Albert's bad habits finally caught up with him. Worn

out with work and worry, he became seriously ill. He developed a stomach ulcer and lost fifty-six pounds in two months. For weeks he lay in bed, overcome with weakness. Sometimes Albert wondered if he was going to die. He was only thirty-eight, but with the general theory of relativity published, he felt he could at least die in peace.

Elsa, however, was determined to nurse Albert back to health. She fed him the most nourishing food she could find and did everything she could to relieve his pain. Thanks to Elsa's care, Albert slowly recovered.

When Germany lost the war in 1918, Albert was relieved. Glad to see the old monarchy replaced by a democratic government, he longed for a country where little boys did not dream of becoming soldiers. He had high hopes that a peace-loving Germany would emerge from the defeat.

He also had hopes for a happy personal life. In 1919, several months after Albert's divorce from Mileva became final, Albert and Elsa were married. It seemed a wonderful arrangement. Albert would always need someone to organize his life, and Elsa clearly loved the job. She was especially happy that Albert adopted her daughters. Although they were twenty-two and twenty years old, Ilse and Margot still lived with their mother. Albert made them his children so they would all feel like a real family.

While Albert was getting used to his new life, he was also thinking of an event that had happened several days before his wedding. On May 29, another solar eclipse had occurred. English scientists who wanted to test Albert's general theory of relativity had observed the eclipse from Brazil and from the island of Príncipe off the coast of West Africa. Einstein was already positive his theory was correct—the mathematical evidence was overwhelming. But for all his certainty, he could hardly wait to hear the results of the expeditions.

Under the direction of Sir Arthur Eddington, a famous English astronomer, the scientists studied their photographs. Carefully they calculated the positions of the stars. Almost four months after the eclipse, Albert received the long-awaited telegram telling him that Eddington had found star displacement at the rim of the sun.

Albert made this cut-out silhouette of his new family shortly after his marriage to Elsa.

This meant that light from the stars had been bent when it passed close by the sun. At last Einstein's theory had been confirmed! Now other scientists could be as certain of the general theory of relativity as Einstein himself had always been.

Although he wrote an excited note to his mother, Albert took the results of the experiment with surprising calm. He hadn't needed proof of his theory—other scientists had. When a student asked him what he would have done if the outcome of the English expeditions had been different, Albert replied with humor and conviction that he would have felt sorry for the Lord, because the theory was indeed correct.

VI

The Most Famous Scientist

The results of the English expeditions were announced on November 6, 1919, in London. All over the world, Einstein's strange and wonderful theory made headlines. Light bent by gravity? Time and space curved around the sun? The incredible ideas captured the public's imagination. Perhaps people needed something to lift their minds from the recent war. Einstein's work was a reminder that the differences between nations were artificial, but the laws of the universe were the same for everyone. The fact that English scientists had confirmed a theory developed in Germany added to the wonder of it all.

Suddenly Albert Einstein was the most famous scientist in the world. At work and at home, reporters clamored to talk to him. Overwhelmed, Albert promised Elsa that soon everything would return to normal, but he was wrong. People named babies after him. Newspapers featured relativity cartoons. A tobacco company even tried to cash in with an Einstein cigar. Within a year, more than one hundred books had been published about relativity. Scientists who wanted to make some extra money lectured on the subject to jammed auditoriums. The magazine *Scientific American* offered a five-thousand-dollar prize for the clearest three-thousand-word explanation of relativity. This was an enormous sum of money in the 1920s. Albert didn't enter the contest. He said he didn't believe he could do it!

The popular enthusiasm for a topic few people could understand amazed Albert. But perhaps the public was even more fascinated by the man than his achievement. In contrast to his complicated work, Albert was really

Einstein being photographed in the 1920s

very simple. His old sarcasm had mellowed into an appealing frankness. He was honest, unworldly, and kind. He was absentminded about things that were not important to him, like brushing his hair or making sure his clothes were pressed. But if something mattered to him, Albert could be quite practical. Reporters who wanted his photograph had to pay him. Then Albert donated the money to buy food for hungry children.

All over Germany, farmlands had been ruined and harvests were small. The economy had collapsed. But the countries that won the war were demanding great sums of money from Germany—money the government didn't have. Until Germany agreed to all the peace terms, the victors wouldn't allow shipments of food from other countries. Children were starving.

Albert's old anger against the land of his birth melted away as he saw the hardship around him. He wanted to do what he could to make Germany a strong, peaceful nation. Finally Albert decided to become a German citizen again. It was a way to support the German people and show his faith in the future.

Some Germans, however, seemed more concerned with the past than the future. They refused to believe their government had been wrong. They tried to blame pacifists and Jews for Germany's defeat. Since he belonged to both groups, Albert became one of their chief targets. An anti-Einstein society was formed to discredit him as a person and as a scientist. It offered large sums of money to people willing to write or speak against Einstein. Some scientists who couldn't understand or accept

Einstein's brilliant theories joined the organization.

In August 1920, a small, bearded man spoke against Albert to a packed concert hall in Berlin. He was twisting Albert's ideas and making relativity sound almost like an evil plot. Suddenly the audience was buzzing with excitement. "Einstein! Einstein!" The whispers rippled rapidly across the room. People nudged one another and stared as Albert slipped quietly into a concert box. To their further amazement, Albert threw back his head and laughed at the ridiculous attacks. He told his friends that the experience was most amusing. But inside, Albert was hurt and angry.

Personal attacks, however bitter or public, could not really tarnish Albert's reputation. Almost any university would have been glad to claim him as a teacher. But some other people were not so lucky. Albert grieved to see many bright, eager students turned away from universities simply because they were Jewish. He was deeply upset to see how difficult it was for Jewish professors to gain appointments. Where could these people go?

Albert began to think more and more about his Jewish heritage. In Prague he had joined the Jewish community to show his support. Now he came to realize the importance of knowledge, justice, and freedom in the Jewish tradition. These were things Albert had valued all his life. He felt drawn to the Zionist movement as a possible solution to the discrimination Jews faced. Zionists wanted to create a country for the Jewish people in Palestine, a land in the Middle East that had belonged to them in biblical times. Albert didn't like the

Einstein with Zionist leader Chaim Weizmann

idea of a separate government for Jews, but he supported the concept of a cultural homeland. He became especially interested in the Zionists' plan for a university where every Jewish scholar would be welcome in Jerusalem, a city in Palestine.

In 1921 Zionists asked Albert to accompany Chaim Weizmann, a leader in the movement, to the United States to raise money for the Hebrew University. Albert still loved solitude. If he went, he would be continually surrounded by people and he would have little time to concentrate on his work. But Albert felt he couldn't say no. He wasn't sure what good his presence on the trip would do, but he knew he had to go.

VII

World Travels

An enthusiastic crowd waited to greet Albert on April 2, 1921, when his ship arrived in New York harbor. Reporters, photographers, and a motion picture crew swarmed aboard. Albert didn't like all the attention, but he was humorous and charming. Reporters liked the middle-aged scientist with the dreamy bright eyes and mop of dark unruly hair. As Albert strode down the gangway with his pipe in one hand and his violin in another, few people could have guessed how much he disliked interviews.

Soon Einstein was attending fund-raising meetings all over the United States. His very presence was an inspiration for America's Jewish population. Scientists and politicians were eager to get close to Einstein too. Several million dollars was pledged to the university during his trip.

Albert and Elsa received a warm welcome when they arrived in the United States on the SS Rotterdam in 1921. Germany and the United States had recently been at war, but the crowd seemed to know Einstein was a man who belonged to all nations.

Albert's warmth and friendliness helped calm the anger some Americans were still feeling toward Germany after World War I. People also liked his independence of spirit. In Boston he was asked to complete a quiz composed by the famous American scientist Thomas Edison. "What is the speed of sound?" read one of the questions. Albert simply shrugged. He didn't know. He said there was no need for him to memorize facts he could find in any textbook. People had to admire Albert for his honesty and bluntness. He might be the genius of the twentieth century, but he was also an ordinary man.

Before Albert returned to Germany, he stopped in England to give several lectures on relativity. Albert knew that anti-German feeling was much stronger in England than in the United States. He hoped his visit would pave the way for better relations between England and Germany. At first people were tense and suspicious when Albert stood up to speak in London. But though he was lecturing about a complicated scientific subject in German, Albert somehow managed to share his courage and his commitment to truth and to peace between nations. After his speech, people rose from their seats and clapped their hands wildly.

Albert's role as a goodwill ambassador continued the next year in March on a scientific trip to France. On the last day of his visit, he went to see some of the World War I battlefields. Albert was shocked at the desolation he found. Whole villages and forests had been destroyed. Albert stared in sorrow. This was something that all young people should see, he said, so that they could understand the ugliness of war.

Shortly after Albert returned home, Walther Rathenau, the German minister of foreign affairs, was murdered. Rathenau was a Jew who believed strongly in international cooperation, and he had been a personal friend of Albert's. Rumors spread that Albert, who shared many of the late minister's beliefs, was next on the list to be killed. Elsa was beside herself with worry. But although Albert canceled an appearance at a scientific conference, nothing could stop him from attending an antiwar demonstration in Berlin that August.

In October Albert and Elsa had a chance to escape from the danger when they set off for a tour of Japan.

Before their ship landed, the 1921 Nobel Prize in physics was announced. Albert had won the award for his work on the photoelectric effect, completed almost fifteen years earlier. (Both relativity theories were still considered too controversial to serve as the basis for the Nobel Prize.) Although he was delighted, Albert wasn't really surprised. He knew he *had* to win someday. He had already promised the prize money to Mileva and his sons.

From Japan Albert and Elsa went to Palestine, where they were greeted warmly and felt instantly at home. Throngs of waving, excited people lined their route as the Einsteins were driven to a special reception at the Lemel School. The mob surged after Albert into the school's courtyard. Gazing at the sea of happy faces, Albert was deeply moved. Never had he identified so strongly with his Jewish roots. He told the enthusiastic crowd that this was the greatest day of his life.

The next day, Albert made the opening speech at the new Hebrew University. Zionist flags decorated the room. A large banner with the Hebrew words for light and learning hung from the ceiling. Albert didn't know Hebrew, but he had studied carefully for this occasion. Slowly he spoke the first sentence of his speech in the Hebrew language. He felt strong bonds of kinship with the people who had come to hear him. Fame had often been a burden. But if fame meant he could help causes like the Hebrew University and share in such historic moments, it was worth the time it took from his research.

After stopping in Spain, Albert and Elsa arrived back in Berlin in February 1923. The latest trip had lasted almost six months, and Albert welcomed the chance for privacy again. He could hardly wait to get back to work. For years he had been trying to develop a unified field theory that would reveal the mathematical relationship between all forces of nature.

In his study in the tower room of his apartment, Albert felt happily alone. If he glanced out the window, all he saw were the rooftops of Berlin and the blue sky. He was surrounded by books, papers, and equations. Even Elsa and his daughters were not allowed in his special retreat.

Sometimes Elsa felt bad that she couldn't dust and organize Albert's study. Albert never minded a little dirt and clutter. What he did mind were the constant demands on his time and attention. Some people wanted money; others wanted Albert to consider their scientific or political ideas. Elsa screened social invitations and requests for interviews. She protected him from the outside world as best she could.

Albert was comfortable with his home life, but he hadn't forgotten his first family. Sometimes Hans Albert and Eduard came to stay with their father in Berlin. Albert often took the ten-hour train ride from Berlin to Zurich to visit Mileva and his sons. In 1923 Hans Albert was a nineteen-year-old engineering student. Tede was thirteen and as eager to learn as his father had always been. But as much as Albert loved his sons, his visits never lasted long. His work was waiting for him at home.

There were also dinner parties and formal academic gatherings. "Feeding time at the zoo," grumbled Albert

Albert, disheveled as usual, playing the violin

when he had to attend. Albert dreaded these occasions. Few things bothered him more than having to get dressed up. But one time he did have some fun in his good clothes. Several friends bet him he couldn't take off his vest without removing his dress coat first. Here was a challenge Albert couldn't resist. He liked clowning around almost as much as he hated dressing up. Albert twisted and turned, he slithered and stretched. Finally he gave a tug, pulled the rumpled vest through his coat sleeve, and burst into laughter.

Like Albert, Elsa had a good sense of humor. One of the family's favorite jokes was to call Albert "the genius." Has the genius returned from work yet? What would the genius like for dinner? No one laughed harder than Albert at the fancy nickname.

In 1928, when he was forty-nine, Albert became ill. Doctors diagnosed a heart condition. He wouldn't be able to return to the university for months. Soon Albert realized that he would need the help of a secretary at home, so Elsa found him a young woman with the necessary skills. At first Helen Dukas was nervous when she met the ailing scientist. Noticing her shyness, Albert grinned up at her from his bed and cracked a joke. Almost instantly, Helen felt at home. The two became close friends.

With Elsa's pampering and Helen's help, Albert slowly regained his strength. By the end of 1930, he was well enough for another trip to the United States. At the California Institute of Technology in Pasadena, Albert looked through the largest telescope in the world. He saw distant galaxies that had recently been discovered. The universe was much bigger than anyone—including Einstein—had imagined. Some of his old ideas would have to be revised. But that was all right with Albert. He never minded admitting he was wrong. And even though the universe was incredibly large, he still believed a single unified field theory could explain it all.

VIII

A Threatening Shadow

It was December 1932, and Albert was troubled as he prepared for his third trip to the California Institute of Technology. The Einsteins were at their vacation home in Germany. Albert loved to go walking through the woods around the old-fashioned village of Caputh. He loved to sail his boat on the nearby lake, standing straight and tall as the wind ruffled his hair and the waves rippled beneath his feet. More than anywhere else in the world, Albert felt at peace in the secluded house he had built shortly after his fiftieth birthday.

But a nagging doubt haunted Albert when he thought about the trip. He told Elsa to take a close look at the villa before they left because it was the last time she would see it.

Elsa was startled. This didn't sound like Albert at all. Usually Elsa was the one who worried while Albert told her everything would be all right. However, recent events

The Einsteins' vacation home in Caputh, Germany

in Germany had cast a threatening shadow over the Einsteins and the country's entire Jewish population. The Nazis, a racist, promilitary political group, were growing in number and attempting to turn public opinion against the Jews. Even in a quiet town like Caputh, the Einsteins' maid had been taunted for working in a Jewish household. These days Elsa did not even like Albert to walk alone in the woods. She was afraid someone would try to harm him. But surely, she told herself, Albert was mistaken about this. Surely they would return next year to enjoy spring in Caputh.

Elsa was wrong. She and Albert were comfortably settled in California when Albert's worst fears were realized. Adolf Hitler came to power in Germany. Hitler blamed

Albert took a spin on his bicycle during his 1933 visit to the California Institute of Technology.

Albert with his son
Hans Albert and
grandson Bernhard
in 1932

the Jews for everything that had gone wrong in Germany.
He believed that Germans with a northern European background, which didn't include Jews and other minorities,
were superior to others. He thought they could prove this
to the world through military strength. Horrified, Albert
and Elsa knew they could never go home while the Nazis
controlled Germany.

In March the Einsteins visited the Institute for Advanced Studies in Princeton, New Jersey. Albert had
accepted a part-time appointment at the institute to begin
that fall. Then the couple set sail for Belgium, where they
planned to spend the summer.

In the past, Albert's music had helped him through difficult times. During the voyage, he used his talent to help

others too. Playing his violin at benefit concerts, he raised money for refugee musicians driven from their homelands by political unrest. In a way, Albert was a refugee too. But he knew that outside Germany he would be welcome almost anywhere in the world.

In the middle of the Atlantic Ocean, the ship received news that a group of Nazis had forced their way into Albert's house in Caputh. Claiming to seek hidden weapons, they even dug up his garden. The only weapon they found in the house was a bread knife. Albert was furious.

One of the first things that Albert did on his arrival in Belgium was renounce his German citizenship for the second time. Then he and Elsa moved temporarily to a small seaside town, Le Coq-sur-Mer. Set in the middle of the village, their house was small and plain, nothing like the pleasant home they missed in Caputh. But joy and relief overshadowed their inconvenience when Ilse and Margot arrived from Paris. Helen Dukas and Albert's assistant, Walther Mayer, also came to Belgium.

In the midst of the cluttered household, Albert continued to work on his unified field theory. He tried to ignore the persistent rumors that his life was in danger from the Nazis. A German album with pictures of Nazi enemies had recently arrived in Belgium. Albert's photograph was on the very first page. The words *Noch Ungehängt,* "not yet hanged," were printed below.

Among Albert's many friends were the king and queen of Belgium. Albert and the queen had often played their violins together. The royal couple was much more frightened about the threat to Albert's life than he was. They insisted on providing him with two bodyguards. They added other precautions too. No one in the neighborhood was supposed to reveal Albert's whereabouts to outsiders.

Albert did not like the idea of detectives guarding his house. He was saddened and angered by the situation in Germany and the way the Germans had treated him. The government had seized his Berlin bank account, sealed his apartment in the city, and taken over his summer house. On May 10, a giant book burning was held in front of the opera house in Berlin. While thousands of people watched and cheered, copies of some of the most powerful books ever written were thrown into the flames, including Albert's works on relativity. Many of the books that were burned were by Jewish authors. Jews were being removed from teaching positions. They were not allowed to practice law or medicine. The Nazis took over Jewish businesses and made it almost impossible for Jews to earn a living.

Albert began to think that giving up his German citizenship was not enough. In view of the terrible events happening in Germany, he felt forced to rethink his views on pacifism. The king of Belgium sent for Albert to discuss the situation with him.

No one knows exactly what Einstein and King Albert said to each other, but they probably discussed the buildup of the German army and the way the country seemed to be preparing for war. In violation of the World War I peace treaty, Germany had begun to build tanks, battleships, and submarines again. The king may also have reminded Albert that Germany had invaded Belgium at the beginning of the First World War.

After these talks, Albert took a different stand on military issues. He said that if he were a Belgian, he would gladly fight. Albert's pacifist friends considered him a traitor to their cause. But Albert feared that only force would be able to stop Germany.

IX

The Atomic Age

In October 1933, Albert and Elsa returned to the United States with Helen Dukas and Walther Mayer. Twelve years earlier, Albert had been swamped with attention when he arrived in New York. This time when his ship entered the harbor, Albert and his party climbed secretly into a tugboat. By the time reporters discovered the trick, Albert was long gone.

The Einsteins rented a house in Princeton and tried to settle into their new surroundings. Albert's new neighbors were proud of his presence in their community. They were curious to know more about him, but they respected his wish for privacy. Outside of Princeton, this wasn't always so. All over the country there were many people who wanted to talk to Albert. He usually turned down all interview requests. The institute also turned down requests for Albert's time—even an invitation for Albert and Elsa to visit President Franklin D. Roosevelt. Such

Albert Einstein and his beloved equations, 1934

a meeting would bring too much publicity, the institute decided.

Albert was upset when he found out about the refusal. Visiting the president was one of the few social activities he *wanted* to do. Immediately he rearranged matters to get a second invitation. In January 1934, Albert and Elsa met President Roosevelt and spent a very enjoyable night at the White House.

Returning from Washington, Albert went on with his calculations. Only a handful of scientists could imagine the mathematical challenges he faced as he continued to develop a unified field theory. Many physicists felt his efforts were doomed to failure. Albert himself admitted the possibility. But he felt he had to try anyway. Besides, he pointed out, his reputation was already made. He could afford to fail, whereas a young, ambitious scientist could not.

There had to be a great law, a scheme that explained everything. Einstein was sure of it, and he was hoping to find it in the unified field theory. Again and again he told friends that he didn't believe God played dice with the world, until it became one of his most famous statements. Albert meant that everything in nature, from the distant galaxies to the particles that make up the atom, is understandable. He firmly believed there was a reason for everything that happened in the universe. Nothing happened by chance.

Yet this was exactly the opposite of what many physicists were saying by the 1930s. They believed that sometimes things did happen for no reason at all. Scientists were beginning to study atoms and the even smaller particles that make up atoms. They performed experiments to see how the particles moved. No matter how much information scientists collected, they couldn't predict the course of an individual particle the same way they predicted the course of a star or planet. Scientists called this phenomenon the uncertainty principle. Albert had no use for uncertainty in science. Nothing could shake his faith in the order of the universe.

But as Europe hastened toward war, tragedy shook Albert's personal life. In 1934 his daughter Ilse died in

Paris of tuberculosis. Elsa, who had gone to Europe to nurse Ilse through her final illness, never got over the loss. When she returned to Princeton with their other daughter, Margot, she was no longer the lively, happy woman she had been. Greatly upset by Ilse's death and his wife's grief, Albert took refuge in his work.

The months passed, and Princeton became home to Albert. He enjoyed his quiet life and his work at the institute. The Einsteins bought a 120-year-old house in a quiet neighborhood near Princeton University. Under Elsa's supervision, part of an upstairs wall was removed and a large picture window was installed. The new bright room overlooked the backyard with its tall shade trees. It had a view all the way down to the college. Elsa knew the room would be a perfect study for her husband.

Soon after the family moved to their new home, Elsa felt her eyes begin to swell. It turned out to be the first symptom of a serious heart and kidney ailment. Over the next year, Elsa grew so sick that Albert didn't want to leave her. He stopped going to his office but continued to work at home. His work was the only relief he got from his anxiety. On December 21, 1936, Elsa died.

Again Albert handled his grief in the only way he knew how. He buried himself in physics. Looking pale and exhausted, he returned to his office and pored over his mathematics.

In the past three years, Albert had become a familiar sight to Princeton townsfolk as he walked to and from his office at the Institute for Advanced Studies. A shabby, but strangely powerful figure with long white hair and

Albert's home in Princeton had green shutters and a covered front porch supported by columns.

bright, gentle eyes, he was the town's very own genius and most talked-about character. Often he seemed lost in thought as he strode down the street in an old sweater and baggy pants. His shoes were scuffed; his ankles bare.

Once some boys asked Albert why he never wore socks. With a smile and a twinkle in his eye, Albert told them he was old enough that if someone told him to put on some socks, he didn't have to listen to them. Albert always had time to talk to the children who greeted him on his walks. Sometimes he tried to impress them by wiggling his ears. Albert considered that a very special talent.

In winter someone drove Albert to work. He never learned to drive himself—he thought it was too complicated. In fact Albert disliked many mechanical things. He didn't use a camera until he was over fifty, and he had trouble with typewriters. But luckily for Albert, he rarely had to bother with these things. When he went home for lunch, Helen Dukas was ready to type up his papers, his statements, or his correspondence. Usually Albert spent his afternoons in his bright back study. He studied his equations, puffed on his pipe, and played his violin when he was stumped.

During the 1930s, more and more people were leaving Europe for the United States and other parts of the world. Albert's son Hans Albert had moved to the United States with his family. Eduard and Mileva were safe in neutral Switzerland.

Many European refugees wrote to Albert to ask for advice and assistance. Albert understood how urgent it was for Jews to leave Germany. He signed affidavits pledging his own money to support Jewish refugees in the United States. Without an affidavit, it was difficult for anyone to get a visa to enter the country. But after signing many such statements, Albert learned that government officials were getting suspicious. They knew he couldn't possibly take care of so many people. Albert stopped signing affidavits, but he continued to seek others willing to help refugees. If he couldn't help someone, Albert always wrote back to offer whatever hope and encouragement he could.

Although Albert wasn't working on his special theory

of relativity these days, some other physicists were taking another look at his famous equation, $E = mc^2$. Years before, during the early 1920s, a young man had told Albert he had used the equation to invent a machine that would make explosives by releasing the energy inside atoms. Albert had told the man his idea was foolish. Now scientists realized such a device might be possible after all.

Two physicists, Otto Hahn and Lise Meitner, had discovered that uranium atoms split in two when they are hit with even smaller particles called neutrons. Energy is released in the process and more neutrons are set free. Scientists believed these neutrons could be used to set off a chain reaction. If the newly freed neutrons hit other atoms, those atoms would break apart too. They would release even more energy and more neutrons. All this would happen so quickly that an explosion would occur. There were still many problems to work out. But if a way could be found to start the reaction and control it, a bomb could be produced that would be millions of times more powerful than an ordinary bomb.

In July 1939, two scientists visited Albert at the cabin on Long Island where he was spending the summer. Leo Szilard and Eugene Wigner brought him up to date on the recent developments in atomic research. Then they shared their fears that if Germany acquired enough uranium, it might be the first country to make the bomb. This would be dangerous for Europe and for the entire free world.

Einstein still had doubts about whether an atomic

bomb could really be made. But even the slight possibility that Germany could develop such a weapon was too horrible for him to think about. At the suggestion of Szilard and Wigner, Einstein signed a letter to President Roosevelt. The letter urged the president to quicken the pace of atomic research and to seek a supply of uranium for the United States. It also said that Belgium's supply of uranium shouldn't be allowed to fall into German hands. In March 1940 Einstein sent two more letters to the president. It was the third letter that influenced the creation of the Manhattan Project. This was the code name for the United States's own intense efforts to develop the bomb.

Albert's sister, Maja, worried about the growing power of the Nazis, came to live with her brother at Princeton in 1939. A few months later, in September, Germany invaded Poland and World War II began. The company of his secretary, sister, and daughter Margot was a great source of comfort to Albert as he followed the war news.

On October 1, 1940, Albert, Margot, and Helen Dukas proudly became American citizens. After the ceremony, Albert joked with reporters, saying he would even give up his sailboat if it were required as a part of his citizenship. One month later, Albert cast his ballot for the reelection of President Roosevelt.

Throughout the war, Einstein knew little of the progress being made on the bomb. Officials did not trust a former German and pacifist with the secrets of atomic research, even if those secrets were based on Einstein's

(Above) Albert and Maja in 1939. The brother and sister looked so much alike that in Princeton people who were used to Albert would turn and stare when they saw Albert and Maja walking together. *(Below)* In 1940 Helen Dukas *(left),* Albert, and Albert's daughter Margot became United States citizens.

own theories. But he did work on one technical problem. Einstein helped devise a way to separate atoms of uranium-235 from slightly heavier atoms of uranium. Uranium-235 is the special form of the element needed to manufacture the bomb.

Albert helped the government in another way too. A fund-raising committee asked him to donate the manuscript of his 1905 paper on the special theory of relativity to be auctioned off. Although Albert had thrown away the original handwritten paper long ago, he offered to create another one. While his secretary read out loud from the published paper, Albert filled page after page. Hearing his own words, he realized how complicated some of them sounded. Surely he could have said certain things more simply, he said. But Albert wrote his second paper exactly like the first. His efforts brought six million dollars to the war effort. Another paper he donated was sold for five and a half million.

Although the war continued against Japan, Germany was defeated in May 1945. The world had known that Jews were being murdered in Germany. But only afterward was the full extent of the tragedy made known. Six million Jewish men, women, and children had died in concentration camps. Sick with grief and rage, Albert never forgave Germany for its crimes.

On August 6, 1945, the United States dropped an atomic bomb on Japan. Helen Dukas heard the news on the radio and told Albert when he came downstairs for tea. Throughout the long, dark years of the war, Albert had believed the conflict could be settled without

Albert spent many happy hours in the bright upstairs study at his Princeton home.

resorting to such a terrible weapon. "Oh weh!" he gasped. It was a cry of sorrow that went beyond words. On August 9, the United States dropped a second bomb on Japan, ending the war.

A new historical era, the atomic age, had been born, and no one knew better than Albert the threat it posed to human survival. For the rest of his life, he worked to make sure the bomb would never be used again. He served on committees to inform the public about atomic energy and the growing danger of weapons development. He supported a world government and warned Americans that the future of civilization depended on international friendship and cooperation.

Albert always found time for children. This picture was taken on Albert's seventieth birthday.

Three years after the war ended, the Jewish state of Israel became a reality at last. Albert was seventy-three years old and in poor health in 1952 when Israel's first president, his friend Chaim Weizmann, died. About a week later, Albert was startled to read in the paper that he was to be offered the presidency of Israel. At first he just laughed. Even when phone calls started coming from United Press and the *New York Times,* he paid little attention.

But that evening, Albert was settling down to dinner when a telegram arrived from Abba Eban. The Israeli ambassador in Washington said he had an important message from Israel.

Instantly Albert knew two things. The newspaper story was true and—as much as he cared about the Jewish people—he could never be president of Israel. In his formal statement, Einstein listed his age, lack of political experience, and the needs of his work as reasons for refusing the offer.

Albert knew he couldn't lead a country. But there *was* something he could still do. With the same old stubbornness and dedication, Albert continued to seek the key to the unified field theory.

All his life Albert loved to sail.

Afterword

Even as an old man, Albert had a sense of fun. On Albert's seventy-sixth birthday, a neighbor gave him a mechanical toy. Albert's face lit up with pleasure as he recognized a playful use of his basic law of gravity. Happily he shared the toy with his visitors. Over seventy years had passed since his father's compass had opened his mind to the mysteries of the universe. The compass had pointed the way to Albert's future. The new toy was a reminder of the past and all that he had accomplished.

Albert wanted to do still more, but weeks later he collapsed when a blood vessel weakened and began to leak. In great pain, he was taken to the hospital. He knew he couldn't live long, but he wanted to make the best use of the time he had left. As soon as his pain lessened, he asked for his spectacles, some paper, and a pen to be brought to the hospital. An unfinished sheet of equations lay by his bed when he died on April 18, 1955.

Albert Einstein's house still stands in Princeton, New

Jersey. Nothing sets it apart from the neighboring homes on the peaceful tree-lined street. This is exactly the way Albert wanted it. He asked that his home not be turned into a museum after he died. He felt it was more important for people to concern themselves with the future than with his memory.

But Albert gave too much to the world to be forgotten. Outside the National Academy of Sciences in Washington there is an enormous statue of Albert. Most statues in the city show people in dignified poses. Albert is shown comfortably sprawled against a half circle of steep concrete steps. The sculptor captured Albert's long hair, his lined face, his casual dress, even his lack of socks. Holding a notebook on his lap, Albert might be relaxing with his equations after a windy sail on a lake or a brisk walk through the woods.

Many scientists now believe that no theory can ever cover all the forces of nature Albert hoped to unite. Other scientists believe some form of unified field theory may be possible. But although Albert didn't succeed in his final quest, perhaps that was not what mattered most in the end.

What really mattered, Albert said toward the end of his life, was to keep on asking questions. Albert was talking to a college student about his own lifelong wonder at the mystery of the universe and about his daily effort to understand a little more of the puzzle. This had always been a joyful, holy task for Albert. Never lose your curiosity, he urged the student.

Albert Einstein never lost his.

Notes

p. 11

A gymnasium was the German equivalent of what we now call a high school.

p. 27

Hans Albert was not Albert and Mileva's first child. A year before the Einsteins were married, Mileva gave birth to a daughter named Lieserl. No one knows exactly what happened to the little girl. In the early 1900s, it was considered scandalous to have a child outside of marriage. Overwhelmed by the situation and Albert's lack of a job, the young couple might not have felt able to take care of Lieserl and probably thought it best to let someone else adopt her.

p. 29

Although Einstein himself didn't pursue the practical implications of his work, other scientists did. Television and fluorescent lights are two inventions that resulted from his work with the photoelectric effect.

p. 29

Some people have suggested that Mileva played a major role in the development of the special theory of relativity. However, Mileva never passed her final exams at the Polytechnic School and never received a degree. Most historians and scientists doubt that Mileva had the mathematical background to make an original contribution to the theory. When Albert occasionally wrote of "our work" to his wife, he was probably referring to her emotional rather than scientific support.

p. 35

Albert often discussed the special theory of relativity with Michele Angelo Besso. His friend was never too tired or busy to listen to Albert. If Michele Angelo did not understand everything, he could at least ask questions. This forced Albert to state his ideas as simply as possible and sometimes to look at them in a new way. Michele Angelo Besso is the only person whose help is acknowledged in the published version of the special theory of relativity.

p. 49

The special theory of relativity dealt only with motion in a straight line at a constant speed. The general theory of relativity dealt with all kinds of movements and took changing speeds and directions into consideration.

p. 51

Albert and Elsa were doubly related. Their mothers were sisters and their fathers were first cousins. Today marriage is often prohibited between such close relatives, but cousins could marry in Germany at this time.

p. 63

Although Albert and Elsa shared a sense of humor and strong loyalty to family and friends, their marriage was not without problems. Unlike her husband, Elsa worried about appearances and other people's opinions. According to some sources, she was sometimes hurt and angered by Albert's behavior. Albert didn't mean to hurt Elsa, but sometimes he found it difficult to see another person's viewpoint. But in his own way, Albert tried to make Elsa happy, and Elsa remained deeply devoted to Albert.

p. 78

Hans Albert Einstein grew up to be a hydraulic engineer. In 1938 he emigrated to the United States with his family, and he eventually became a professor at the University of California at Berkeley. He enjoyed occasional visits with his father. Eduard Einstein developed a mental illness as a young man and was never able to complete his education at the University of Zurich. Albert last saw his younger son in 1933 just before moving to Princeton. Eduard lived with Mileva in Zurich until her death in 1948, after which he went to live in a health-care facility.

Bibliography

Bucky, Peter A., in collaboration with Allen Weakland. *The Private Albert Einstein.* Kansas City: Andrews & McMeel, 1992.

Calder, Nigel. *Einstein's Universe.* 2d ed. New York: Greenwich House, 1982.

Clark, Ronald W. *Einstein: The Life and Times.* 2d ed. New York: Avon Books, 1984.

Dukas, Helen, and Banesh Hoffman, eds. *Albert Einstein: The Human Side: New Glimpses from His Archives.* Princeton, N.J.: Princeton University Press, 1987.

Einstein, Albert. *The Collected Papers of Albert Einstein. Vol. 1, The Early Years, 1879–1902.* Trans. Anna Beck. Princeton, N.J.: Princeton University Press, 1987.

Einstein, Albert. *Ideas and Opinions.* 2d ed. New York: Crown Publishers, Inc., 1982.

Einstein, Albert. *Out of My Later Years.* rev. ed. Secaucus, N.J.: The Citadel Press, 1956.

Einstein, Albert. *Relativity: The Special and General Theory.* New York: Crown Publishers, Inc., 1959.

Einstein, Albert. *The World As I See It.* Trans. Alan Harris. New York: The Citadel Press, 1984.

Frank, Philipp. *Einstein: His Life and Times.* Trans. George Rosen. Ed. Shuichi Kusaka. New York: Da Capo Press, Inc., 1989.

French, A. P., ed. *Einstein: A Centenary Volume.* Cambridge, Mass.: Harvard University Press, 1979.

Hoffman, Banesh, with the collaboration of Helen Dukas. *Albert Einstein: Creator and Rebel.* New York: The Viking Press, 1972.

Jones, Roger S. *Physics for the Rest of Us.* Chicago: Contemporary Books, 1992.

Lerner, Aaron B. *Einstein & Newton: A Comparison of the*

Two Greatest Scientists. Minneapolis: Lerner Publications Company, 1973.

Michelmore, Peter. *Einstein, Profile of the Man.* New York: Dodd, Mead, & Co., 1962.

Miller, William. "Old Man's Advice to Youth: Never Lose a Holy Curiosity." *Life* (May 2, 1955).

Pais, Abraham. *'Subtle is the Lord...' The Science and the Life of Albert Einstein.* New York: Oxford University Press, 1982.

Reiser, Anton. *Albert Einstein: A Biographical Portrait.* London: Thornton Butterworth Limited, 1931.

Sayen, Jamie. *Einstein in America: The Scientist's Conscience in the Age of Hitler and Hiroshima.* New York: Crown Publishers, Inc., 1985.

Schwartz, Joseph, and Michael McGuinness. *Einstein for Beginners.* New York: Pantheon Books, 1979.

Seelig, Carl. *Albert Einstein: A Documentary Biography.* Trans. Mervyn Savill. London: Staples Press Ltd., 1956.

Vallentin, Antonina. *The Drama of Albert Einstein.* Trans. Moura Budberg. Garden City, N.Y.: Doubleday & Co., Inc., 1954.

White, Michael, and John Gribben. *Einstein: A Life in Science.* New York: Dutton, 1994.

Whitrow, G. J., ed. *Einstein: The Man and His Achievement.* New York: Dover Publications, Inc., 1973.

Zee, A. *An Old Man's Toy: Gravity at Work and Play in Einstein's Universe.* New York: Macmillan Publishing Co., 1989.

Index